A to Z Israel

BY JUSTINE AND RON FONTES

children's press®

A Division of Scholastic Inc.
New York Toronto London Auckland Sydney
Mexico City New Delhi Hong Kong
Danbury, Connecticut

Consultant: Simone Ribke
Series Design: Marie O'Neill
Photo Research: Candlepants Incorporated

The photos on the cover show the Dome of the Rock (right), a Sabra cactus (bottom), a Jewish girl holding kittens (middle), and a dolphin (left).

Photographs ©2003: AllSport USA/Getty Images/Nathan Bilow: 8 top; Art Resource, NY/The Jewish Museum, New York, NY: 17 right; Corbis Images: 15 left (AFP), 33 (Dave Bartruff), 25 top (Annie Griffiths Belt), 13, 15 right, 23 top right (Bettmann), cover bottom, 17 left (Shai Ginott), cover center (Robert Holmes), 37 left (Hanan Isachar), 4 bottom, 5 top left, 5 bottom, 19, 35 top (Steve Kaufman), 22 right (David Lees), 6 top, 16 top, 24 top, 28 bottom, 37 right, 38 top (Richard T. Nowitz), 10 top, 12 top, 23 left (ReutersNewMedia Inc.), 12 bottom, 34 top (David Rubinger), 36 center (Moshe Shai), 9 left, 23 bottom right (Ted Spiegel), 26 (The Dead Sea Scrolls Foundation, Inc.), 32 (Underwood & Underwood), 10 bottom, 36 right; Corbis SABA/Ricki Rosen: 16 bottom, 28 top; Corbis Sygma: 14; Envision Stock Photography Inc.: 11 left, 34 bottom, 38 bottom (Steven Needham), 10 right (Osentoski & Zoda); Getty Images: cover top left (Ian Cartwright), 18 (Richard T. Nowitz/National Geographic Image Collection); Index Stock Imagery/ASAP Ltd.: 5 top right, 6 bottom, 9 right, 24, 29, 30; PhotoDisc/Getty Images: 35 bottom (Neil Beer), 9 center (Steve Cole); PictureQuest/Steve Allen/Brand X Pictures: cover top right; Robertstock.com: 27 (Steve Allen), 22 left (R. Opfer), 36 left (Zefa); Stone/Getty Images/R. Kord: 25 bottom; Taxi/Getty Images/John Downer: 4 top; The Image Bank/Getty Images: 7 (Gary Cralle), 31 (Stephen Frink); The Image Works/Carl Glassman: 8 bottom.
Maps by XNR Productions

Library of Congress Cataloging-in-Publication Data

Fontes, Justine.
    Israel / by Justine and Ron Fontes.
        p. cm. – (A to Z)
    Includes bibliographical references and index.
    Summary: Provides an introduction to Israel's culture, geography, history, economy, government, and more.
    ISBN 0-516-24560-0 (lib. bdg.)   0-516-26811-2 (pbk.)
    1. Israel–Juvenile literature. 2. Israel–Description and travel
 –Juvenile literature.   [1. Israel.]   I. Fontes, Ron. II.
Title.
    III. Series: Fontes, Justine. A to Z.
DS118.F65 2003
956.94'003–dc21

                                    2003005837

1 2 3 4 5 6 7 8 9 10 R 12 11 10 09 08 07 06 05 04 03

Contents

Animals

Many of Israel's animals can live in deserts or mountains. Camels are suited to live in a dry, sandy place.

Ibex

The Fennec, a small desert fox, sleeps during hot days and hunts at night. Fennecs eat large insects, mice, birds, lizards, and sweet fruits.

The oryx is an antelope with long, straight horns.

Camels have been around since prehistoric times. Arabian camels have one hump. Bactrian camels have two. Its hump stores fat that the camel can live on if there is no food or water.

Other animals that live in Israel are the ostrich and ibex. The ostrich is the largest living bird. Ostriches can't fly, but they can run about 40 miles (64 km) per hour!

The ibex is a kind of wild goat that lives in the mountains. Their horns grow to be around 4 feet (1.2 m) long.

Ostrich

Jerusalem's Dome of the Rock is a holy place to Muslims.

Buildings

Many modern buildings sprang up after Israel became the Jewish homeland in 1948.

Israel's buildings show its long history. There are many ruins that date back to Biblical times. Others were built by the Ancient Romans or by Arabs who lived there.

Many buildings in Israel's capital, Jerusalem, are sacred sites to Jews, Christians, or Muslims.

Jerusalem's Old City

Cities

Jerusalem is Israel's capital and largest city. A thick wall surrounds the Old City, which is at the heart of modern Jerusalem.

The Old City has a Jewish Quarter, or neighborhood, and an Arab Quarter. The Western Wall is in the Jewish Quarter. It is the most sacred site in the Jewish religion. The Arab Quarter is full of narrow streets and open-air markets.

Dress

Many Israelis wear modern clothes like suits, T-shirts, and shorts. Some wear clothes that express their religious faith.

Hasidic men have been dressing the same way since the 16th Century.

Kippah & Yarmulke

(kee-PAH)   *(YAH-muh-kuh)*
mean skullcap

Many Jewish men wear skullcaps or **kippahs** as a sign of respect for God. The Yiddish word for kippah is **yarmulke**. Yiddish is a Jewish language that mixes Hebrew, German, and other European languages. **Hasidic** people are very religious. Hasidic men wear big fur hats and long coats.

Some Muslim women wear a long veil, or burkha, when they are out in public. The burkha prevents strangers from seeing their face and body.

Israel imports uncut diamonds from South Africa, then exports cut diamonds all over the world.

Exports

Israel's biggest export is cut diamonds. Skilled workers turn rough stones into shiny gems that can be made into jewelry.

Israel also exports fruits, vegetables, and flowers. Jaffa oranges are famous all over the world. Sweet, thick-skinned oranges have been grown in the port city of Jaffa for hundreds of years.

Salat Gezer Recipe

WHAT YOU NEED:
- 3 carrots grated (about 2 cups)
- juice of 1-2 oranges, about 1/2 cup
- juice of 1 lemon, about 1/4 cup
- 1/4 cup honey
- fresh mint leaves

HOW TO MAKE IT:
Put carrots in a bowl. Stir in juices and honey. Cover and refrigerate for at least two hours. Garnish with mint before serving.

Food

Israeli cooking is a mixture of Middle Eastern and European Jewish recipes. Many public places serve **kosher** food. Kosher means "fit" or "proper" according to Jewish law. Meat and milk are never served at the same meal or even on the same plates.

Israelis love to eat fresh foods like salat gezer, or carrot salad. Ask an adult to help you make salat gezer using this recipe.

11

Today's president, Moshe Katsav (left), is Israel's eighth president. Here, President Katsav meets with Prime Minister Ariel Sharon (right).

Government

Golda Meir

The Israeli Parliament is called the **Knesset**. Israelis 18 and older vote to elect the 120 members of the Knesset.

The members of the Knesset vote to select Israel's president, or nasi. The nasi serves a five-year term and attends public events, but does not make important decisions. The prime minister is elected by the people and leads the Israeli government.

In 1969, Golda Meir became Israel's first and only female prime minister. She was prime minister for five years.

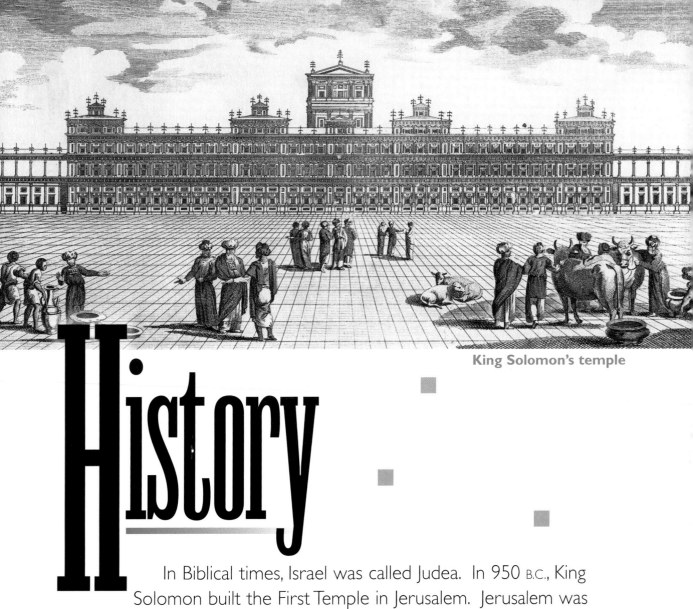

King Solomon's temple

History

In Biblical times, Israel was called Judea. In 950 B.C., King Solomon built the First Temple in Jerusalem. Jerusalem was destroyed by the armies of Rome in A.D. 70 and the Jews were scattered all over the world. This is called the **Diaspora**.

During the 19th century, a movement called **Zionism** started. Zionists worked to create a Jewish homeland. Many Zionists moved to the land, which was then called Palestine. During the 1930s more Jewish people came to Israel to escape the German **Nazis** in Europe.

On May 14, 1948, Israel became an independent nation and was made their homeland. Since then it has fought many wars with its Arab neighbors.

Achinoam Nini, or Noa, started singing at age three.

Important People

Israel has been the home of many great writers. It has also inspired musicians, dancers, painters, and other artists.

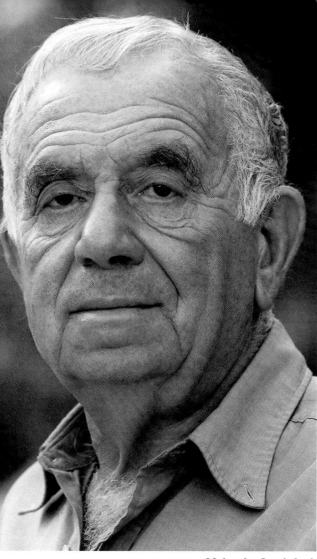

Yehuda Amichai

S.Y. Agnon

Yehuda Amichai's family moved to Israel from Germany when he was 11 years old. Yehuda fought in World War II and then in the Israeli Army. He wrote poems about tanks, airplanes, and other everyday subjects.

S.Y. Agnon was born in Poland, but came to Israel at age nine. At 15, his poems were published in a newspaper. Agnon went on to earn the highest honor in writing, the Nobel Prize, for his novels, stories, and poems.

Jobs

Israel's computer and high tech industries are growing.

Many Israelis used to work on farms. Today most farm work is done by machines, and most now have service jobs in which they help other people.

They also work in the tourist industry, and for the government. Some train new **immigrants** for work in Israel. Others build housing for the immigrants.

Some olive wood carvings are of religious subjects, but many are of animals.

Mezuzah

Keepsakes

A great keepsake is a **mezuzah**. They contain a verse from the **Torah**, the Jewish Bible. Many doorways in Israel have mezuzahs. Whenever religious Jewish people enter or leave a building, they touch the mezuzah on the doorpost. You can buy them with covers made of everything from plastic to gold.

You can't bring an olive tree home, but you can buy things made from it like small sculptures and jewelry.

Land

Israel is only the size of the state
of New Jersey, but it has mountains,
deserts, valleys, and plains.

All summer long, Israel receives little or no rain. During the winter, lots of rain falls in the north. There is less rain in the south. Much of the southern half of Israel is the Negev Desert. Many farms in Israel must be **irrigated** in order to grow crops.

The Jordan River is Israel's most important river. It connects with the Sea of Galilee in the northeast, and with the Dead Sea in the east.

Mayim

(MAH-yeem)
means water.

Map

LEBANON

SYRIA

Sea of Galilee

Golan Heights

Haifa

Mediterranean Sea

Tel Aviv

West Bank

Jordan River

N
W E
S

Jerusalem

Dead Sea

Gaza Strip

ISRAEL

JORDAN

Negev Desert

EGYPT

ISRAEL

MILES
0   80

KILOMETERS
0   80

Red Sea

SAUDI ARABIA

Nation

Magen Daveed

(mah-GEN dah-VEED)
means Star of David.

The flag of Israel started as the flag of the World Zionist Organization. The Zionists were working to create a Jewish nation. It became the flag of Israel when the nation was founded in 1948. The colors come from Jewish prayer shawls, which are white with blue stripes on the edges. The 6-pointed star in the middle of the flag is the Star of David, a symbol of the Jewish people.

Jews come from all over the world to pray at the Western Wall.

Muslims pray five times each day. This Meuzzin is calling Muslims to pray.

Only in Israel

The three largest religions in the world all have their roots in Jerusalem.

Jerusalem's Church of the Nativity was built where Christians believe Christ was born.

Church of the Holy Sepulcher in Jerusalem.

The Dome of the Rock contains the stone from which Muslims believe Mohammed rose to heaven when he died. He claimed to hear the voice of God.

In 1000 B.C., King David made Jerusalem the capital of his Kingdom. David's son, King Solomon, built a temple there. This First Temple was destroyed. In 516 B.C., a new temple was built on the same spot. It was also destroyed. All that is left is its Western Wall.

The most sacred site for Christians is also in Jerusalem. It is the Church of the Holy **Sepulcher**, the place where Jesus is believed to have been buried and then rose from the dead. A sepulcher is a tomb.

People

Many Jewish people, now living in Israel, came from other countries. There are also many Arabs who stayed in their homes after Israel was formed

Israelis speak many different languages. Hebrew is the official language. Many people also speak English. Some speak the languages of their native countries, like Russian or Ethiopian.

Many Israelis live in modern apartment buildings in cities like Tel Aviv and Haifa. Most of Israel's Arab people live in farm villages, or in Arab neighborhoods in Israel's cities and towns.

Question

What are the Dead Sea Scrolls?

Before there were books, people wrote on sheets of paper stuck together to form one long roll or scroll. Scribes copied scrolls by hand. In Ancient Israel, scribes copied the Old Testament, which contains the first 39 books of the Bible.

In 1947, an Arab shepherd found some old clay pots in a cave near the Dead Sea. The pots held scrolls with parts of the Old Testament and other historical documents. These became known as the Dead Sea Scrolls. Scholars were very excited because these are the oldest known copies of the Old Testament.

The Star of David

Religion

Israel is the only country in the world where Judaism is the major religion. Four out of five Israelis are Jewish, but many are not religious.

Most of the non-Jewish people living in Israel are Arab Muslims. There are also some people called Druzes who practice a different part of the Islamic faith. There are small numbers of Christians and people who practice other religions.

Israeli law protects the freedom of religion and all sacred sites.

School & Sports

The government provides Israeli children with a free education until they are 17. In Israel, children attend school six days a week. Most schools teach in Hebrew.

Israelis enjoy sports too. They like water sports such as swimming, surfing, and sailing. They also play soccer, tennis, and basketball.

Israel has a worldwide sporting event much like the Olympics. It is called the Maccabiah, and Jewish people come from all over the world to compete in its many events. The first Maccabiah was held in 1932.

Transportation

There is about one car for every five people in Israel. Most people travel by bus. Tel Aviv has the world's largest bus station.

El Al is Israel's official airline. Ben-Gurion International Airport, near Tel Aviv-Jaffa, is Israel's main airport. There are several smaller airlines that travel within Israel and to neighboring countries.

Israel has three major deep water seaports: Haifa, Ashdod, and Eilat.

Unusual Places

The Dead Sea is the lowest place on Earth! The water is too salty for fish and other sea life to live in and it's ten times saltier than normal seawater.

People visit the Dead Sea to float in its mineral-rich water. People also enjoy soaking in hot springs and black mud baths to ease aching muscles and bones, and to nourish their skin. The air near the Dead Sea has more oxygen than anywhere else on Earth.

Coral is a tiny animal that lives in warm oceans. They live in colonies. Their skeletons form giant reefs. A reef is a ridge of rock or coral near the surface of the sea. Many beautiful, tropical fish live in coral reefs.

Snorkeling is a great way to explore coral and other things in the ocean. The facemask keeps your eyes dry. The snorkel lets you breathe without having to lift your head out of the water. The rubber fins help you swim fast, like a fish.

Visiting the Country

Window to the Past

The Western Wall, or **Kotel**, is all that remains of the Temple in Jerusalem. These ruins have become a symbol of Jewish survival.

Many people place written prayers in the cracks in the Western Wall.

The Bible says that King Solomon built the First Temple in Jerusalem. That temple was destroyed about 2,600 years ago. King Herod rebuilt a second temple on the same spot. When the Romans destroyed Jerusalem in A.D. 68, the Second Temple was also ruined. Only the Western Wall remained standing. Today, Jewish people come from all over the world to pray at the Western Wall.

X-tra Special Things

Hummus

Geckos are lizards. The smallest gecko that lives in Israel is smaller than many insects!

One special place is Israel's Kidron Valley. It has hundreds of ancient tombs. Some of the burial chambers are carved into the rocky cliffs. These date from the time of the First Temple built by King Solomon.

Hummus is good food! It is a dip made from chick peas, lemon juice, sesame paste, oil, and spices. People enjoy it with pita bread, cut vegetables, and many other foods. Hummus has been eaten since ancient times.

Another place you can visit is the Dead Sea. Many people who go there smear themselves with its black mud. The mud has minerals that are good for skin. Special shampoos, soaps, and facial masks are made from Dead Sea salt and mud.

The shofar is a horn blown on the Jewish New Year in September or October.

This girl is dressed like a clown for Purim.

Menorah

Yearly Festivals

Most Israelis celebrate the same holidays as many Jewish people celebrate all over the world. They celebrate both religious and national holidays.

During the harvest holiday of Sukkot, Jews decorate a hut or booth with fruits and vegetables. Sukkot means booth.

A man waving the Israeli flag on Independence Day

In late November or early December, Israelis celebrate Hanukkah, the Festival of Lights. Hanukkah recalls when the Jewish people pushed the Syrians out of Israel and took back the temple in Jerusalem.

The Jewish people lit a lamp that had only enough oil for one day, but the lamp burned for 8 days! Today candles are lit in a special holder called a **Menorah** for the 8 days of Hanukkah.

Purim is another celebration. Queen Esther was a beautiful Jewish woman married to a Persian King. The King's evil advisor, Haman, convinced the King to kill all the Persian Jews. But Esther saved her people!

During Purim whenever Haman's name is mentioned, Jewish children spin noisemakers called **graggers**.

Olive Trees

Zayteem

Zayteem are olives. Olives can grow in poor soil where other plants can't survive.

Olive trees bloom in the spring and are ready to harvest in the fall. Some olive trees are thought to be over 1,000 years old! The green fruit turns black when it is ripe. There are many different kinds of olives. Some are used for eating, others are pressed to make olive oil.

Some Jewish people use oil-burning Menorahs during Hanukkah in memory of the oil used by the early Jews in their temples.

Hebrew and English Words

Diaspora (dee-AS-puh-ruh) the departure of Jews from Judea during the 8-6th centuries B.C.

gragger (GRAH-ger) a noisemaker spun by Jewish children during Purim

Hasid (HAH-sid) a member of a very religious group of Jews

immigrant (IM-uh-gruhnt) a person who moves to another country to settle

irrigate (IHR-uh-gate) to bring water to crops using pipes, channels or other means

kippah (kee-PAH) Hebrew word for the skullcap worn by religious Jewish males

Knesset (kuh-NESS-et) Israel's parliament

kosher (KOH-sher) food prepared according to Jewish law

Kotel (KOH-tel) the Western Wall, all that remains of the ancient Jewish temple in Jerusalem

Magen Daveed (mah-GEN dah-VEED) the Star of David, the symbol of the Jewish people

mayim (MAH-yeem) Hebrew word for water

menorah (muh-NOR-uh) a 9-branched candle holder used by Jews to celebrate Hanukkah

mezuzah (meh-ZOO-zuh) a religious text in a case attached to the doorpost of Jewish homes as a sign of faith

Nazi (NAHT-see) a member of Adolf Hitler's German National Socialist Party, which killed millions of Jews, Gypsies, and other people while ruling Germany from 1933-1945

sepulcher (SEH-puhl-kuhr) a room or cave built to hold the dead

shofar (shoh-FAR) a ram's horn trumpet sounded during Jewish religious ceremonies

sukkot (soo-COTE) Hebrew word for booth, also the name of a harvest holiday in which booths are decorated with crops

Torah (TOR-uh) the first five books of the Bible written in Hebrew

yarmulke (YAH-muh-kuh) Yiddish word for skullcap

zayteem (ZAY-teem) Hebrew word for olives

Zionism (ZYE-uh-niz-im) the movement to establish Israel as a Jewish homeland

Let's Explore More

Israel (Food and Festivals) by Ronne Randall, Raintree, 1999

The Dead Sea: The Saltiest Sea (Great Record Breakers in Nature) by Aileen Weintraub, Powerkids Press, 2001

Ticket to Israel by Marcia S. Gresko, Carolrhoda Books, 2000

Websites

www.gemsinisrael.com/kids.htm
Visit some of Israel's less famous sites, like a Monkey Park between Jerusalem and Tel Aviv.

www.jeru.huji.ac.il
Learn about the history of Israel by following this timeline -- includes recipies, costumes, and a virtual tour of sites around Israel.

www.jeru.huji.ac.il/md/vjt
Take a virtual tour of Jerusalem on this Web site.

Index

Italic page numbers indicate illustrations.

Meet the Authors

JUSTINE & RON FONTES have written nearly 400 children's books together. Since 1988, they have published *critter news*, a free newsletter that keeps them in touch with publishers from their home in Maine.

The Fonteses have written many biographies and early readers, as well as historical novels and other books combining facts with stories. Their love of animals is expressed in the nature notes columns of *critter news*.

During his childhood in Tennessee, Ron was a member of the Junior Classical League and went on to tutor Latin students. At 16, Ron was drawing a science fiction comic strip for the local newspaper. A professional artist for 30 years, Ron has also been in theater as a costumer, makeup artist, and designer.

Justine was born in New York City and worked in publishing while earning a BA in English Literature Phi Beta Kappa from New York University. Thanks to her parents' love of travel, Justine visited most of Europe as a child, going as far north as Finland. During college, she spent time in France and Spain.